LifeChange

A NAVPRESS BIBLE STUDY SERIES

*A life-changing
encounter with God's Word*

WOMEN OF THE NEW TESTAMENT

*Disciples of Jesus love and lead in ways
that challenge cultural norms and
transform communities.*

NavPres

T0014619

A NavPress resource published in alliance
with Tyndale House Publishers

NavPress is the publishing ministry of The Navigators, an international Christian organization and leader in personal spiritual development. NavPress is committed to helping people grow spiritually and enjoy lives of meaning and hope through personal and group resources that are biblically rooted, culturally relevant, and highly practical.

For more information, visit NavPress.com.

Women of the New Testament: A Bible Study on How Followers of Jesus Transcended Culture and Transformed Communities

Copyright © 2023 by The Navigators. All rights reserved.

A NavPress resource published in alliance with Tyndale House Publishers

NavPress and the NavPress logo are registered trademarks of NavPress, The Navigators, Colorado Springs, CO. *Tyndale* is a registered trademark of Tyndale House Ministries. Absence of ® in connection with marks of NavPress or other parties does not indicate an absence of registration of those marks.

Written by Joyce Koo Dalrymple

The Team:
David Zimmerman, Publisher; Caitlyn Carlson, Acquisitions Editor; Elizabeth Schroll, Copy Editor; Olivia Eldredge, Operations Manager; Sarah Susan Richardson, Designer, Sarah K. Johnson, Proofreading Coordinator

Cover photograph of terracotta pots copyright © CamBuff/Getty Images. All rights reserved.

Author photo by Stephen Hong, copyright © 2019. All rights reserved.

For information about special discounts for bulk purchases, please contact Tyndale House Publishers at csresponse@tyndale.com, or call 1-855-277-9400.

ISBN 978-1-64158-662-7

Printed in the United States of America

29	28	27	26	25	24	23
7	6	5	4	3	2	1

CONTENTS

HOW TO USE THIS STUDY

Objectives

The topical guides in the LifeChange series of Bible studies cover important topics from the Bible. Although the LifeChange guides vary with the topics they explore, they share some common goals:

1. to help readers grasp what key passages in the Bible say about the topic;

2. to provide readers with explanatory notes, word definitions, historical background, and cross-references so that the only other reference they need is the Bible;

3. to teach readers how to let God's Word transform them into Christ's image;

4. to provide small groups with a tool that will enhance group discussion of each passage and topic; and

5. to write each session so that advance preparation for group members is strongly encouraged but not required.

Each lesson in this study is designed to take forty-five minutes to complete.

Overview and Details

The study begins with an overview of the women of the New Testament. The key to interpretation for each part of this study is context (what is the referenced passage *about*?), and the key to context is purpose (what is the author's *aim* for the passage as it relates to the overall topic?). Each lesson of the study explores the story of one or more women in the New Testament with a corresponding passage from the Bible.

Kinds of Questions

Bible study provides different lenses and perspectives through which to engage with the Scripture: observe (what does the passage *say*?), interpret (what does the passage *mean*?), and apply (how does this truth *affect* my life?). Some of the "how" and "why" questions will take some creative thinking, even prayer, to answer. Some are opinion questions without clear-cut right answers; these will lend themselves to discussions and side studies.

Don't let your study become an exercise in knowledge alone. Treat the passage as God's Word, and stay in dialogue with Him as you study. Pray, *Lord, what do You want me to see here?*, *Father, why is this true?*, and *Lord, how does this apply to my life?*

It is important that you write down your answers. The act of writing clarifies your thinking and helps you to remember what you're learning.

Study Aids

Throughout the guide, there are study aids that provide background information on the passage, insights from commentaries, and word studies. These aids are included in the guide to help you interpret the Bible without needing to use other, outside resources. Still, if you're interested in exploring further, the full resources are listed in the endnotes.

Scripture Versions

Unless otherwise indicated, the Bible quotations in this guide are from the New International Version of the Bible. The other version cited is the English Standard Version.

Use any translation you like for study—or preferably more than one. Ideally you would have on hand a good, modern translation such as the New International Version, the English Standard Version, the New Living Translation, or the Christian Standard Bible. A paraphrase such as *The Message* is not accurate enough for study, but it can be helpful for comparison or devotional reading.

Memorizing and Meditating

A psalmist wrote, "I have hidden your word in my heart that I might not sin against you" (Psalm 119:11). If you write down a verse or passage that challenges or encourages you and reflect on it often for a week or more, you will find it beginning to affect your motives and actions. We forget quickly what we read once; we remember what we ponder.

When you find a significant verse or passage, you might copy it onto a card to keep with you. Set aside five minutes each day just to think about what the passage might mean in your life. Recite it to yourself, exploring its meaning. Then, return to the passage as often as you can during the day for a brief review. You will soon find it coming to mind spontaneously.

For Group Study

A group of four to ten people allows for the richest discussions, but you can adapt this guide for other-sized groups. It will suit a wide range of group types, such as home Bible studies, growth groups, youth groups, and workplace Bible studies. Both new and experienced Bible students, and new and mature Christians, will benefit from the guide. You can omit or leave for later any questions you find too easy or too hard.

The guide is intended to lead a group through one lesson per meeting. This guide is formatted so you will be able to discuss each of the questions at length. Be sure to make time at each discussion for members to ask about anything they didn't understand.

Each member should prepare for a meeting by writing answers for all the background and discussion questions to be covered. Application will be very difficult, however, without private thought and prayer.

Two reasons for studying in a group are accountability and support. When each member commits in front of the rest to seek growth in an area of life, you can pray for one another, listen jointly for God's guidance, help one another resist temptation, assure each other that each person's growth matters to you, use the group to practice spiritual principles, and so on. Pray about one another's commitments and needs at most meetings. If you wish, you can spend the first few minutes of each meeting sharing any results from applications prompted by previous lessons and discuss new applications toward the end of the meeting. Follow your time of sharing with prayer for these and other needs.

If you write down what others have shared, you are more likely to remember to pray for them during the week, ask about what they shared at the next meeting, and notice answered prayers. You might want to get a notebook for prayer requests and discussion notes.

Taking notes during discussion will help you remember to follow up on ideas, stay on the subject, and have clarity on an issue. But don't let note-taking keep you from participating.

Some best practices for groups:

1. If possible, come to the group discussion prepared. The more each group member knows about the passage and the questions being asked, the better your discussion will be.

2. Realize that the group leader will not be teaching from the passage but instead will be facilitating your discussion. Therefore, it is important for each group member to participate so that everyone can contribute to what you learn as a group.

3. Try to stick to the passage covered in the session and the specific questions in the study guide.

4. Listen attentively to the other members of the group when they are sharing their thoughts about the passage. Also, realize that most of the questions are open-ended, allowing for more than one answer.

5. Be careful not to dominate the discussion—especially if you are the leader. Allow time for everyone to share their thoughts and ideas.

6. As mentioned previously, throughout the session are study aids that provide background information on the passage, insights from commentaries, and word studies. Reading these aloud during the meeting is optional and up to the discussion leader. However, each member can refer to these insights if they found them helpful in understanding the passage.

A Note on Topical Studies

LifeChange guides offer robust and thoughtful engagement with God's Word. The book-centric guides focus on a step-by-step walk through that particular book of the Bible. The topical studies use Scripture to help you engage more deeply with God's Word and its implications for your life.

INTRODUCTION

Women of the New Testament

WOMEN ARE EVERYWHERE IN THE NEW TESTAMENT. They follow and serve Jesus, seek Him for healing, and play creative and essential roles in the early church. Motivated by love, these women are honest and persistent, often defying cultural gender norms in their pursuit of Jesus. Their bold faith, displayed by their words and deeds, disrupts a male-dominated world.

For much of our history since, however, their stories have been mediated and interpreted through a male-centric lens, which often misses these disruptions. This may mean that you will be surprised when you see what an active and courageous role women played in the days when Jesus and His apostles announced the arrival of the Kingdom of God, and the role Jesus continues to invite all His disciples into today.

In this LifeChange study guide, we will study how Jesus welcomes marginalized and culturally neglected people as disciples, publicly affirms their faith as examples for others, and empowers them to lead and use their gifts. We will also allow the women's words to speak for themselves as they follow Jesus and tell others about Him:

- "I am the Lord's servant. May your word to me be fulfilled." —Mary (Luke 1:38)

- "If I just touch his clothes, I will be healed." —the woman who had been bleeding for twelve years (Mark 5:28)

- "Lord, Son of David, have mercy on me!" —the Canaanite woman whose daughter was demon possessed (Matthew 15:22)

- "I believe that you are the Messiah, the Son of God, who is to come into the world." —Martha, after her brother Lazarus died (John 11:27)

- "Come, see a man who told me everything I ever did." —the Samaritan woman at the well (John 4:29)

- "I have seen the Lord!" —Mary Magdalene, the first witness of the Resurrection (John 20:18)

As Jesus reveals Himself to these women, they express a remarkable understanding of His identity and mission. Throughout their interactions with Jesus, women are seen, empowered, and commissioned by their Savior in powerful ways. Alongside men, they generously give and serve and teach and lead in ways that help spread the gospel. As we consider these extraordinary women, may we all—men and women alike who follow Jesus—be inspired by their stories, draw closer to Jesus in wholehearted devotion, follow Him in countercultural ways, and partner together to transform communities.

MARY AND ELIZABETH

Luke 1:39-56

THE BEGINNING OF LUKE INTRODUCES us immediately to two women, who at the time the Gospels were written were unlikely main characters in the grand story of God's redemption. It "invites the reader into the world of [Mary and Elizabeth] and begins the story of Jesus from their perspective."[1] Elizabeth comes from the priestly line of Aaron and marries Zechariah, who is himself a priest. She lives a life of righteousness and integrity (Luke 1:5-6) but carries the lifelong societal disgrace of being childless. Mary, on the other hand, is a young virgin, probably between twelve and fourteen years old, who is betrothed to be married to Joseph. Imagine her surprise when the angel Gabriel visits her and tells her that she is "highly favored" and will give birth to the promised Messiah (verses 28-33). Though Mary must have many questions, her response is full of faith: "I am the Lord's servant. May your word to me be fulfilled" (verse 38).

The angel tells Mary that her cousin Elizabeth, even at her advanced age, is with child. Mary immediately makes the long journey from Nazareth to the hill country of Judea to see her. Elizabeth's child would be John the Baptist, the prophet who would prepare the way for Jesus. Despite their differences in age and situation, Mary and Elizabeth find refuge and strength in one another while God is literally growing something new and miraculous inside each of them. They powerfully affirm and bless the work of God to each other through prophecy.

The events that take place in the beginning of Luke are not just important for Mary and Elizabeth personally but constitute a pivotal point in the story of God's relationship with His chosen people—and ultimately in the fulfillment of God's salvific purposes not only for the Jews but also for the entire world.[2]

1. Read Luke 1:39-45. As soon as Elizabeth hears Mary's greeting, the baby leaps inside her womb and Elizabeth immediately understands the imminence of the Messiah's birth. Before Mary can explain what has happened to her, Elizabeth, full of the Holy Spirit, speaks words of affirmation and blessing to Mary. When has someone spoken words of affirmation from God that you needed to hear? How did that impact your ability to move forward in your calling?

_____

_____

_____

_____

_____

_____

_____

_____

_____

"Nowhere can we better see the paradox of blessedness than in the life of Mary. To Mary was granted the blessedness of being the mother of the Son of God. Well might her heart be filled with a wondering, tremulous, amazed joy at so great a privilege. And yet that very blessedness was to be a sword to pierce her heart. . . . Some day she would see that Son of hers hanging on a cross."[3]

2. Elizabeth says several times that Mary is blessed (verses 42-45). In what ways is Mary blessed?

_____

_____

_____

_____

_____

_____

_____

_____

3. When God is birthing something new, a person can feel vulnerable because others cannot see the growth yet. Elizabeth's prophetic blessing enables Mary to sing her own prophetic song. Similarly, as God's people, we are called to "spur one another on toward love and good deeds" (Hebrews 10:24). What is a specific way you can do that for someone who needs encouragement right now?

_____

_____

_____

_____

_____

_____

_____

_____

_____

4. Read Luke 1:46-56, which is known as the Magnificat (from the Latin word for "magnifies"). What stands out to you as you read Mary's song?

_____

_____

_____

_____

_____

_____

_____

_____

_____

Mary "lived in an honor/shame culture." A girl who was betrothed but not yet married and who became pregnant could be stoned. Even if God protected her from that, Mary knew she and her son "would probably always live with some kind of social stigma as to His legitimacy and the true story behind her pregnancy."[4]

5. Mary's words are profound in the face of what she is about to do. She doesn't express fear of what others will think of her; rather, she rejoices. What leads her to rejoice in verses 46-49?

_____

_____

_____

_____

_____

_____

_____

_____

_____

_____

6. The scope of the Magnificat points back to God's mercy extending to Abraham and his descendants forever and forward to God's saving work through Christ. Who receives mercy and help in verses 50-55?

_____

_____

_____

_____

_____

_____

_____

_____

_____

_____

7. These words depict God's revolutionary vision for the world. Describe what Mary's song reveals about God's values versus the world's values.

_____

_____

_____

_____

_____

_____

_____

_____

_____

_____

_____

8. How does the baby in Mary's womb come to fulfill the words of Mary's song in His ministry and in the Kingdom He ushers in?

_____

_____

_____

_____

_____

_____

_____

_____

_____

_____

_____

New Testament scholar Scot McKnight writes that "five of the major themes of Jesus' very own teachings and mission" are found in the Magnificat. First, Jesus "hallows God's Name, prays for daily bread, and blesses the hungry." Second, He "blesses the poor and opens banquet doors to the poor. . . . He frequently shows mercy to widows." Third, Jesus "regularly tussles with unjust powers." Fourth, Jesus "is known for mercy and compassion." Fifth, Jesus prays over and longs for the redemption of Jerusalem.[5]

9. During the three months that Mary stays with Elizabeth, the elder Elizabeth must be mentoring her young cousin. Elizabeth is probably an ideal mentor for Mary since, after years of barrenness, she is also experiencing the fulfillment of God's promises. What preparation do you need in this season? What steps can you take to pursue a mentor to help equip you in that preparation?

_____

_____

_____

_____

_____

_____

_____

10. Mary and Elizabeth submit themselves to God and experience deep joy and deep sorrow as they watch their sons grow up and fulfill God's mission in ways they do not expect. When you say yes to following Jesus, you follow Him one step at a time, not knowing all the challenges that will come in the journey. What might help you say yes to God's calling for you, despite the uncertainty and difficulties you may face?

_____

_____

_____

_____

_____

_____

_____

_____

Your Response

If you were to write a song to God right now, what kind of song would you write? Would it be a song of rejoicing like Mary's or a song of lament or longing? Take ten minutes to write out a stanza or two to God, looking to the Magnificat or the Psalms for inspiration.

For Further Study

Hannah's song has been called the Magnificat of the Old Testament. Hannah experiences despair in her childlessness, but God rewards her faith by granting her a son she names Samuel. Samuel becomes the last judge and a powerful prophet who anoints the first two kings of Israel. Read 1 Samuel 2:1-10. How are Mary's and Hannah's songs similar?

_____

_____

_____

_____

_____

_____

_____

_____

_____

_____

_____

_____

_____

_____

_____

_____

_____

THE SAMARITAN WOMAN

John 4:1-42

AFTER THE ASSYRIANS CONQUERED the northern kingdom of Israel in 721 BC and took away many captives, some of the Jews stayed behind and intermarried with the Assyrians. These people became known as the Samaritans. The Samaritans had their own unique version of the first five books of Scripture, as well as their own unique system of worship. The Jews and the Samaritans strongly disagreed about the proper place of worship, whether at the Temple in Jerusalem or atop Mount Gerizim in Samaria. Jews considered Samaritans racially and ritually unclean and avoided interactions with them.

But Jesus, as we might expect, was different. In John 4, Jesus passes through Samaria on His way from Judea in the south to Galilee in the north. Many Jews on the same journey would endure a much longer route, going around Samaria to avoid the Samaritan people. Jesus, however, plunges straight into Samaria, seeks out a Samaritan woman at a well, and asks her for a drink. He then proceeds to offer her water that leads to eternal life so that she will never thirst again.

The Samaritan woman is curious and open, posing intelligent and theologically astute questions. What ensues is the longest recorded conversation Jesus has with any individual in the Bible. The Samaritan woman goes from calling Him "sir" (verse 11) to identifying Him as a prophet (verse 19) to understanding that He is the Messiah (verses 25-26, 29). She models discipleship in her growing understanding of who Jesus is, and her response to this revelation is to evangelize her people. She partners with Jesus in transforming her community before even the disciples understand what Jesus is talking about.

The Samaritan woman points out the significance of this well—that it originated with "our father Jacob" (verse 12). Jacob is a common ancestor for Jews and Samaritans.

1. Where and when does Jesus sit down to rest from His journey (verses 4-6)?

_____

_____

_____

_____

_____

_____

_____

_____

_____

_____

_____

Some scholars argue that morally upright women drew water in the morning when it was cooler, suggesting that the Samaritan woman was immoral and thus had to draw water alone in the middle of the day. But New Testament professor Lynn Cohick casts doubt on this interpretation: "Notice John doesn't say why the woman was at the well at noon. . . . Maybe she needed more water to finish her tasks. John tells us the time of day to explain why Jesus would be hot and tired, not to comment on when virtuous women drew water."[1]

2. Read John 4:1-42. Count the number of exchanges Jesus and the Samaritan woman have from verses 7 to 26. Why do you think dialogue is a more effective way than "preaching" to connect with the Samaritan woman?

_____

_____

_____

_____

_____

_____

_____

_____

_____

_____

3. Jesus initiates the conversation with the Samaritan woman by asking her for a drink. Why is the Samaritan woman surprised that He asks *her* for a drink (verse 9)? What kind of barriers is Jesus crossing in doing so?

Under Jewish law, even a Samaritan water vessel was considered unclean for Jewish drinking.[2] Often in Scripture (see Genesis 24:10-51; 29:1-20; Exodus 2:15-21) when an unmarried man goes to a well to ask a woman for a drink, it can suggest that the man is seeking a bride.[3]

_____

_____

_____

_____

_____

_____

_____

_____

_____

_____

4. Jesus piques the woman's interest by telling her about a different kind of water that He can give her. Describe the extraordinary nature of the water that Jesus offers this woman in verses 10 and 13-14 (see also John 7:37-39).

_____

_____

_____

_____

_____

_____

_____

_____

_____

_____

_____

Cohick writes that Jesus does not label the Samaritan woman as sinful or tell her to "go and leave your life of sin," as He commands the adulterous woman in John 8:11. The Samaritan woman is unlikely adulterous because no man would dare marry a convicted adulteress. It is also unlikely that she is a serial divorcee because she would need the repeated help of a male advocate to initiate a divorce. Perhaps one or two of her marriages ended in divorce. Cohick suggests it is more likely her five marriages and current arrangement are the results of unfortunate events that took the lives of several of her husbands.[4]

5. How does Jesus treat the Samaritan woman? What might be surprising or unexpected about what He does with His knowledge of her marital history and current cohabitation?

_____

_____

_____

_____

_____

_____

_____

_____

_____

_____

6. Rather than using His knowledge of the Samaritan woman's relationships with men to condemn her, Jesus uses it to reveal His identity. How does Jesus' knowledge of the Samaritan woman's life lead her to recognize who He is (verses 19, 29, 39)?

_____

_____

_____

_____

_____

_____

_____

_____

_____

7. The Samaritans worshiped on Mount Gerizim and the Jews worshiped in Jerusalem. Jesus, however, makes worshiping at a physical location irrelevant, stating that "true worshipers will worship the Father in the Spirit and in truth" (verses 23-24). What does worshiping the Father in Spirit and in truth mean?

_____

_____

_____

_____

_____

_____

_____

_____

_____

Skye Jethani, an author, pastor, and podcast host, asserts that "truth" here is not just about espousing the correct doctrine about God but is also about "worshiping God out of the truth of who we are," coming to God in honesty.[5] The woman at the well began the conversation by hiding the truth that she'd had five husbands and the one she was living with was not her husband. By His grace, Jesus revealed that He fully knew her history and offered her, a Samaritan woman, the gift of eternal life.

8. How does redefining worship in this way change our human expectations about what it means to access God?

_____

_____

_____

_____

_____

_____

_____

_____

_____

_____

"A more exact translation would be 'I am, the one speaking to you.'... The Samaritan woman heard the first 'I am' in John. The clear declaration of Jesus' identity given to the woman contrasts with the questions throughout the rest of the Gospel.... Jesus' self-revelation to the woman sets her story apart from most others."[6]

9. The Samaritan woman says that she is expecting the Messiah to come to explain everything. Jesus responds, "I who speak to you am he" (verse 26, ESV). This is the first time Jesus clearly announces His identity as the Messiah in the Gospels. Why do you think Jesus chooses to reveal who He is to a Samaritan woman?

_____

_____

_____

_____

_____

_____

_____

_____

_____

_____

10. The disciples return and are confused as to why Jesus has been talking to a Samaritan woman and whether Jesus has eaten. What food has Jesus eaten that He says the disciples know nothing about (verses 27-37)?

_____

_____

_____

_____

_____

_____

_____

_____

_____

_____

11. After Jesus reveals His identity, the Samaritan woman leaves her water jug and immediately goes to tell the people in her town about Jesus (verse 28). Jesus does not even officially commission her to go before she has become an effective evangelist, reaping a great harvest in her town. In contrast, Jesus has to command His disciples, "I tell you, open your eyes and look at the fields! They are ripe for harvest" (verse 35). What "fields" are around you? Where might you be missing an unexpected harvest of those who need to hear the good news about Jesus?

_____

_____

_____

_____

_____

_____

_____

_____

_____

_____

_____

_____

_____

_____

_____

_____

_____

_____

Your Response

The crux of the Samaritan woman's testimony is that Jesus knows everything she's ever done. He knows her deepest pain and desires and personally extends salvation to her. Jesus also knows everything about you and offers you His amazing grace and unconditional love. What invitation do you think Jesus is extending to you right now? How do you want to respond to His invitation?

_____

_____

_____

_____

_____

_____

_____

_____

_____

_____

_____

_____

_____

_____

_____

_____

_____

_____

_____

For Further Study

Read the story of Nicodemus in John 3:1-21.
Nicodemus is a knowledgeable teacher, a
Pharisee, and a member of the Jewish ruling
council. What differences do you observe
between how Nicodemus and the Samaritan
woman respond to Jesus?

THE BLEEDING WOMAN

Mark 5:21-43

TWELVE STRAIGHT YEARS. That's how long this unnamed woman in Mark 5 has been hemorrhaging. In her world, according to Jewish purity laws, women are unclean and cannot enter the Temple while they are menstruating. In the Bible, the number twelve can symbolize completeness. This woman lives in a complete and ongoing state of uncleanness that equals religious isolation.

This woman probably feels forgotten or invisible after suffering with this condition for so long. Her inability to participate in the full religious experience of her people has perhaps come to define her identity. Scripture does not give her a name; maybe her community has forgotten it as well. Perhaps the people around her know her only as the bleeding or unclean woman.

Desperate to be healed, this woman has spent all her money on doctors, but instead of getting better, she has only gotten worse (Mark 5:26). Yet she hasn't given up. Even after twelve years of trying everything she can, when she hears that Jesus is in town, somehow she has faith that He may be the answer to her prayers. She courageously ventures out into the crowd to meet Him.

1. Describe a time when you were in a desperate situation and had exhausted all your options. What did you do?

_____

_____

_____

_____

_____

_____

_____

_____

2. Read Mark 5:21-43. The narrative of the bleeding woman is sandwiched between the beginning and end of the story of Jairus's daughter. What differences do you notice between the bleeding woman's situation and that of Jairus's daughter (verses 25, 42; Luke 8:42)? What similarities?

In Judaism, girls come of age at twelve years old. Jairus's daughter dies before her father can marry her off, receive a dowry, and expect grandchildren to continue his lineage. Seminary professor Mary Ann Getty-Sullivan explains: "Thus the father may have faced financial loss as well as social disgrace, in addition to the personal sorrow of his daughter's illness and death."[1]

_____

_____

_____

_____

_____

_____

3. Jairus is a synagogue ruler and a prominent figure in the community who publicly requests that Jesus come heal his daughter. In contrast, the bleeding woman has no advocate, stays hidden in the crowd, and approaches Jesus discreetly from behind. Why do you think she does not directly approach Jesus and ask Him to heal her (verse 27)?

_____

_____

_____

_____

_____

_____

_____

4. The woman thinks, "If I just touch [Jesus']
clothes, I will be healed," and "immediately
her bleeding stop[s]" (verses 28-29). Based on
Luke's and Matthew's accounts, the woman
must be crouching on the ground, because she
touches the hem of Jesus' cloak (Matthew 9:20;
Luke 8:44). What do these thoughts and actions
indicate about the woman's faith?

_____

_____

_____

_____

_____

_____

_____

_____

_____

"Grace is shockingly
personal. As Henri
Nouwen points out, 'God
rejoices. Not because the
problems of the world
have been solved, not
because all human pain
and suffering have come
to an end, nor because
thousands of people have
been converted and are
now praising him for his
goodness. No, God rejoices
because *one* of his children
who was lost has been
found.'"[2]

5. Jesus keeps looking for the woman who has
touched His cloak, which the disciples think is
strange because the crowd is pressing in around
Him and many people must have touched Him
(verses 30-32). Why do you think Jesus does not
give up until He finds the woman?

_____

_____

_____

_____

_____

_____

_____

_____

_____

6. The disciples may think Jesus' delay is jeopardizing "the mission" of going to heal Jairus's only daughter, who is at the point of death. Jesus eventually heals the daughter of the powerful man, but He prioritizes the woman who has no advocate. How can focus on "the mission" sometimes prevent us from seeing and caring for the vulnerable? What steps can you or your community take to prioritize the needs of those on the margins?

_____

_____

_____

_____

_____

_____

_____

7. The woman cannot worship in the Temple because based on purity laws, she is considered unclean, and touching others will make them unclean too. But when she encounters God in the flesh, the opposite happens: Jesus makes her clean. Sometimes our circumstances make us want to hide from God and others. In what ways can receiving the grace of Jesus help you let go of shame and turn toward the God who desires to heal you and make you clean?

Author and psychiatrist Curt Thompson writes that "when we experience shame, we tend to turn away from others because the prospect of being seen or known by another carries the anticipation of shame being intensified or reactivated.... [But] shame's healing encompasses the counterintuitive act of turning toward what we are most terrified of.... It is in the *movement toward another*, toward connection with someone who is safe, that we come to know life and freedom from this prison."[3]

_____

_____

_____

_____

_____

_____

_____

Author Aubrey Sampson writes: "Jesus spoke a blessing and new name over her. . . . No longer 'a woman having an issue of blood.' Defined by isolation. Defined by shame. Instead, 'Daughter.' Defined by relationship. Defined by belonging. Defined by wholeness."[4]

8. The woman falls at Jesus' feet and tells Him the whole story, perhaps seeking mercy. What is Jesus' response (verses 33-34)?

_____

_____

_____

_____

_____

_____

_____

_____

_____

"The Greek for 'healed' [sesōken] can also mean 'saved.' Here both physical healing ('be freed from your suffering') and spiritual salvation ('go in peace') are probably meant. The combination of physical and spiritual healing also occurs in 2:1-12 . . . 3:1-6."[5]

9. The woman has already been physically healed when Jesus speaks the words "Daughter, your faith has healed you. Go in peace and be freed from your suffering" (verse 34). What further healing occurs when Jesus speaks?

_____

_____

_____

_____

_____

_____

_____

_____

_____

10. In asking the woman to be vulnerable and
    courageously step forward, Jesus expands her
    physical healing into a holistic healing. Describe
    a time when you began to experience healing
    because you shared what you went through with
    those who listened and cared.

Your Response

Jesus is interested in healing the whole person. The woman seeks Jesus out for physical healing, but Jesus pursues her to heal her emotionally, socially, and spiritually. What kind of healing are you seeking, and what kind of healing do you think Jesus wants to give you? What steps can you take to pursue this healing?

_____

_____

_____

_____

_____

_____

_____

_____

_____

_____

_____

_____

_____

_____

_____

_____

_____

_____

_____

For Further Study

Even after the woman's bleeding stops, Jesus keeps searching for her until she is found. Throughout the Bible, God pursues His people so that they can be in close relationship with Him. Read the parables of the lost sheep, the lost coin, and the lost son in Luke 15. What does the main character (God) rejoice in, and what does this reveal about God's heart toward you?

_____

_____

_____

_____

_____

_____

_____

_____

_____

_____

_____

_____

_____

_____

_____

_____

_____

_____

THE CANAANITE WOMAN

Matthew 15:21-28

THE CANAANITES WERE THE "most morally despised of Israel's enemies in the Old Testament."[1] They were a culture who practiced child sacrifice, temple prostitution, and other atrocities. The Canaanites lived in the land before Abraham arrived, and God had ordered their destruction and the demolition of their idols in the Old Testament (see Numbers 33:50-55; Deuteronomy 7:1-11).

This longstanding enmity makes the story of the woman in Matthew 15 particularly striking. She is not only a Gentile but a Canaanite. In the Gospel of Mark, this Canaanite woman is referred to as the Syrophoenician woman because she was born in Syrian Phoenicia (Mark 7:26). Risking rejection and humiliation, this woman courageously crosses ethnic, religious, and gender barriers to beg Jesus to heal her daughter.

Like the bleeding woman, she has probably exhausted all her options. She has heard about Jesus healing people. Perhaps she has even heard that Jesus has healed the centurion's servant (Matthew 8:5-13). The fact that the centurion is also a Gentile may give her hope that maybe Jesus will have mercy on her, too. In any case, when she hears that Jesus has come to the region of Tyre and Sidon, she seeks Him out. She does not care what others think of her. Her daughter is demon possessed, and this mother is desperate. Her mother's heart gives her courage and persistence to do everything she can for her daughter.

1. Read Matthew 15:21-28. What stands out to you about the Canaanite woman?

_____

_____

_____

_____

_____

_____

_____

_____

_____

_____

_____

2. This woman's love for her daughter motivates her to cross social, ethnic, gender, and religious barriers in approaching Jesus. While you may not have encountered these same kinds of barriers, we have all had to overcome obstacles in our lives to pursue something important to us. Describe a time when you persevered to overcome an obstacle. What did you learn from that experience?

_____

_____

_____

_____

_____

_____

_____

_____

_____

_____

Canaanites did not recognize the title "Son of David" because Jews reserved it for the Messiah, the legitimate king of Israel. By acknowledging Jesus as the "Son of David," this woman is also recognizing the right of the kingdom of David over the land.[2]

3. The Canaanite woman cries out, "Lord, Son of David, have mercy on me!" (verse 22). Why would her use of that particular title be significant?

_____

_____

_____

_____

_____

_____

_____

_____

_____

_____

Jesus' statement to the disciples is a repetition of the limited commission He gives them in Matthew 10:6 to go to the lost sheep of Israel. But before Jesus ascends to heaven, He extends the commission for the disciples to be His witnesses "in Jerusalem, and in all Judea and Samaria, and to the ends of the earth" (Acts 1:8). The order of places where the disciples would witness reflects the way the gospel would spread first to the Jews, then to the Gentiles. God's plan for salvation from the very beginning has included all people: God promised to bless Abraham and all peoples through him (Genesis 12:1-3) and called Israel a light to all nations (Isaiah 49:6). Through the Cross, Jesus fulfilled His ultimate mission, to unite Jews and Gentiles into one entity and reconcile both to God (Ephesians 2:14-18).

4. What do you think Jesus means when He tells the disciples that He has been "sent only to the lost sheep of Israel" (verse 24)?

_____

_____

_____

_____

_____

_____

_____

_____

_____

_____

_____

_____

_____

5. Undeterred, the woman comes closer to Jesus. What do her posture and words in verse 25 reveal about her?

_____

_____

_____

_____

_____

_____

_____

_____

_____

_____

6. Instead of quietly sending this suffering woman away, Jesus appears to insult her by comparing her to a dog. It was not unusual at that time for Jews to refer to Gentiles as dogs. What do you think Jesus means by His comment that "it is not right to take the children's bread and toss it to the dogs" (verse 26)?

Commentators disagree as to what Jesus means here. Some assert that He is testing or bantering with her. Others say that the Greek form for the word "dog" is diminutive, referring to a household pet rather than a stray dog. Still others suggest that Jesus is comparing her to a group of philosophers at that time called Cynics, "who rejected certain cultural expectations, and because of that, people referred to them as dogs." Jesus' words could be linking her to these boundary-breaking philosophers, perhaps even in a positive way.[3] Or perhaps Jesus is holding up a mirror to the disciples of how Jewish culture views this woman before upending their cultural biases by rewarding her faith.

_____

_____

_____

_____

_____

_____

_____

_____

_____

_____

"Jesus has told her a parable in which he has given her a combination of challenge and offer, and she gets it. She responds to the challenge: . . . She says, 'All right. I may not have a place at the table [as a non-Jew]—but there's more than enough on that table for everyone in the world, and I need mine now.' She is wrestling with Jesus in the most respectful way and she will not take no for an answer. . . .
" . . . This is rightless assertiveness, something we know little about. She's not saying, 'Lord, give me what I deserve on the basis of my goodness.' She's saying, 'Give me what I *don't* deserve on the basis of *your* goodness—and I need it now.'"[4]

Each time the Canaanite woman addresses Jesus, she calls Him "Lord," acknowledging Him as her master. She asks Him to "have mercy" (verse 22), to "help" her (verse 25), and for "crumbs that fall from [the] master's table" (verse 27). Her words display a heart of humility, faith, and boldness.

7. How does the woman's response—"even the dogs eat the crumbs that fall from their master's table"—demonstrate her understanding of what Jesus is doing (verse 27)?

_____

_____

_____

_____

_____

_____

_____

_____

8. In the passage preceding the story of the Canaanite woman, the Pharisees and teachers of the law criticize Jesus for breaking purity rituals (verses 1-2). Jesus responds that they are hypocrites who focus so much on following tradition that their religion has become heartless (verses 3-9). He explains that it is not what goes inside a person's mouth that defiles a person but rather what comes out, because that reflects the evil in their hearts (verses 16-20). Based on what comes out of this woman's mouth, how would you describe her heart?

_____

_____

_____

_____

_____

_____

_____

_____

_____

9. Why do you think Jesus appears to change His mind and grant her request (verse 28)?

_____

_____

_____

_____

_____

_____

_____

_____

_____

_____

_____

Jesus praises her for her "great faith." In contrast, only a chapter earlier, Jesus rebuked Peter's "little faith" (14:31). Peter left the boat in the first place because he wanted proof of Jesus' presence: "If it's you, tell me to come to you on the water" (14:28). There is no "if" in the woman's statement that Jesus is the Son of David.[5] Moreover, Peter began to sink when he saw the adversity of the situation, whereas the woman persists in the face of setbacks.

10. In Mark's account of the same story, the woman takes Jesus at His word when He says her request has been granted. She then ends the conversation and goes home to find her daughter healed (see Mark 7:29-30). Describe a situation where you need to take Jesus at His word and believe His promise for you.

_____

_____

_____

_____

_____

_____

_____

_____

_____

_____

Your Response

Out of love for her daughter, this woman
is unwilling to take Jesus' silence or initial
resistance as a no. She does not care how she will
be perceived by others; she humbly persists in her
intercession and reverses the situation. Have you
been tempted to give up when your prayers seem
to go unanswered? What can you learn from this
woman to help you persevere? Take some time to
share and pray about a request to God that has yet
to be answered.

_____

_____

_____

_____

_____

_____

_____

_____

_____

_____

_____

_____

_____

_____

_____

_____

_____

_____

For Further Study

Read the story in Matthew 8:5-13 about Jesus
healing the centurion's servant. What similarities
do you notice between the Roman centurion and
the Canaanite woman? What do the concluding
words of both stories have in common?

MARTHA

John 11:17-35

MARTHA IS OFTEN REMEMBERED FOR complaining that her sister, Mary, was not helping her in the kitchen (Luke 10:38-42).[1] In that story, Martha invites Jesus and His disciples to her home but grows distracted by all the domestic preparations. Her sister, Mary, simply sits at the feet of the teacher. Exasperated, Martha pleads with Jesus, "Don't you care that my sister has left me to do the work by myself? Tell her to help me!" (verse 40).

But Jesus cares more about the state of Martha's heart than whether the food is perfectly prepared. He lovingly points out that she is "worried and upset about many things" and invites Martha to see Mary in a new light (verse 41). Jesus doesn't ask Martha to stop using her amazing gift of hospitality, but He does want to free her from seeking her worth through society's expectations of her. Jesus shows her that He is the only Savior who can meet her deepest need.

While Martha's response to Jesus is not recorded in the Gospel of Luke, I believe Martha takes Jesus' words to heart because she later turns to Jesus in her deepest time of need: after her brother Lazarus dies. Instead of being distracted by her duties as she was before, here Martha receives Jesus' words, focuses on who He is, and gives one of the clearest confessions of faith in the Gospels. Martha makes a remarkable transformation from complaining to Jesus about things not going her way to trusting in Jesus after the loss of her loved one.

1. Read John 11:4-7, which explains Jesus' delay in going to heal Lazarus. What stands out to you in these verses?

_____

_____

_____

_____

_____

_____

_____

_____

_____

_____

2. Read verses 17-28. As soon as Martha hears that Jesus is coming, she breaks with custom (to remain in the house) and goes to meet Him. Martha's first words to Jesus are bold and honest: "Lord, if you had been here, my brother would not have died" (verse 21). What do these words reveal about her faith and her disappointment?

"According to custom, members of the family were supposed to remain mourning for the first seven days (unless perhaps going to weep at the tomb)," while others visited their home to provide food and consolation.[2]

We can guess what Martha is thinking through the words she says. "Martha would have liked to say: 'When you got our message, why didn't you come at once? And now you have left it too late.'"[3]

_____

_____

_____

_____

_____

_____

_____

Lament is a way we can relate to God in our pain. Over one-third of the Psalms are lament Psalms. Pastor Mark Vroegop writes, "Lament is the honest cry of a hurting heart wrestling with the paradox of pain and the promise of God's goodness."[4]

3. By the time Jesus arrives, Lazarus has been dead for four days. We have all faced loss, grief, and disappointments in life. Describe how experiencing loss has affected your relationship with God.

_____

_____

_____

_____

_____

_____

_____

_____

_____

Now Jesus, having been raised to life, is at the right hand of God interceding for us (Romans 8:34).

4. Martha follows her statement of disappointment with an incredible expression of faith in verse 22: "But I know that even now God will give you whatever you ask." While she does not know what Jesus is about to do (see verse 39), *even now*, after Lazarus has already died, Martha trusts that Jesus will go to the Father to intercede on her behalf. Do you believe that Jesus is your advocate even when circumstances feel hopeless? How can you practically live out that belief?

_____

_____

_____

_____

_____

_____

_____

_____

5. Jesus shares the gospel in verses 25-26. How would you explain these verses to someone who is not a Christian?

_____

_____

_____

_____

_____

_____

_____

_____

_____

_____

_____

6. How does Martha's response to Jesus reveal her faith in who He is (verse 27)?

_____

_____

_____

_____

_____

_____

_____

_____

_____

_____

_____

7. Compare Martha's reaction to Mary in Luke 10:40 to her words to Mary in this passage (John 11:28). In what ways has Martha been transformed through her relationship with Jesus?

_____

_____

_____

_____

_____

_____

_____

_____

_____

_____

8. Read John 11:29-35. Compare and contrast Mary's response to seeing Jesus with Martha's.

_____

_____

_____

_____

_____

_____

_____

_____

_____

_____

9. Even though the sisters say the same thing to Jesus, He engages with them differently. How does He respond to Mary, and what does this reveal about Jesus (verses 33-35)?

_____

_____

_____

_____

_____

_____

_____

_____

_____

_____

_____

_____

_____

_____

_____

_____

_____

_____

_____

_____

_____

_____

"Even though Jesus knew he could restore Lazarus to physical life, he wept with sorrow and sympathy. Here, the word 'wept' did not refer to the wailing that customarily accompanied funerals in that day . . . often done by people who did not know or care about the dead person."[5]

Scholar Allie Ernst writes that in John's Gospel, "the confession of Jesus as the Christ is placed not on the lips of Peter, but on those of Martha. Is her confession of 'the Messiah, the Son of God' then the rock upon which the Johannine church is founded? And if so, what might this reveal about the place of women in the Johannine communities on the one hand and the place of Martha in early Christian traditions on the other?"[6]

Your Response

Martha and Mary both begin by telling Jesus how they feel. Then, accepting Jesus' words, Martha chooses to affirm her trust in who He is. At times you need to grieve (for however long it takes), but eventually, you face a choice of whether to trust Jesus and let Him comfort you. If you are grieving a loss, take some time to journal, pray, or share with others and bring your grief honestly before the Lord. You may even pray, *Lord, if you had been here, _____ would not have died.* If you're not experiencing loss right now, what are some ways you can be a supporting presence to those who are?

_____

_____

_____

_____

_____

_____

_____

_____

_____

_____

_____

_____

_____

_____

_____

_____

_____

_____

_____

For Further Study

Read Matthew 16:13-19. How does Peter's confession of who Jesus is in Matthew 16:16 compare to Martha's confession in John 11:27? What is Jesus' response to Peter's statement (Matthew 16:17-19)?

MARY OF BETHANY

John 12:1-7

MARY OF BETHANY, the sister of Martha and Lazarus, appears three times in the Gospels by name—and each time, we find her at Jesus' feet. Mary does not have as many speaking lines as Martha in these stories, but her heart of worship becomes clear through her actions.

First, Mary breaks with tradition by sitting at Jesus' feet to soak in His every word (Luke 10:38-42). When Martha complains that Mary should be working with her instead, Jesus affirms Mary's choice. He says that only one thing is needed and Mary has chosen what is better. Mary shows up again after her brother, Lazarus, dies. In the rawness of her grief, she runs to Jesus and falls at His feet, crying, "Lord, if you had been here, my brother would not have died" (John 11:32). She brings her broken heart to Him. Though He knows He will raise Lazarus from the dead, He is so moved by her mourning that He weeps.

In this session, we focus on Mary's final appearance in the Gospels, where she boldly interrupts a dinner party to anoint Jesus' feet. Once again, she comes to Jesus as she is, bringing her whole self and all that she has to offer. Mary does not care that she is breaking social norms, because her sole focus is on loving Jesus. In her last recorded encounter with Jesus, perhaps knowing that this may be one of the last times she will see her Lord, Mary again comes to His feet, pouring out her heart in an extravagant act of devotion.

---

1. Read John 12:1-7. What words or phrases stand out to you?

_____

_____

_____

_____

_____

_____

_____

_____

_____

_____

_____

_____

_____

2. In this dinner given in Jesus' honor, Martha is serving Jesus, Lazarus is reclining at the table with Jesus, and Mary is kneeling at Jesus' feet (verses 2-3). Describe your current posture toward Jesus. In what ways do you want your posture to change?

_____

_____

_____

_____

_____

_____

_____

_____

_____

_____

"It was common to anoint the heads of important guests, but for their feet a host normally would simply provide water. Expending such expensive perfume on feet was shocking; [Mary] treats even Jesus' feet as worthier than a normal head."[1] One prophetic connection is that it was Jewish custom to anoint a body with oil before burial.

3. It is almost Passover, and Jesus is preparing to enter Jerusalem, where the chief priests and Pharisees are looking to arrest and kill Him. In what ways does Mary's anointing His feet with perfume and wiping them with her hair prepare Jesus for the suffering He is about to face?

_____

_____

_____

_____

_____

_____

_____

_____

_____

"Because such ointment would have been so expensive, scholars often think that [Mary's perfume] was a family heirloom. In any case, it represented nearly a year's wages for an average worker and would be reserved for only a dramatically special occasion."[2]

In contrast to how much Mary values Jesus' worth, Judas only values Jesus at thirty pieces of silver. That's how much he gets paid for turning Jesus over to the chief priests (Matthew 26:14-15). In Hebrew culture, thirty pieces of silver was not a lot of money. Thirty shekels (or about twelve ounces) of silver was the exact price paid to the master of a slave when his slave was killed by a bull (Exodus 21:32).

4. Read how Judas and the others respond to Mary's actions (verses 4-6; see also Matthew 26:8-9; Mark 14:4-5). Taking care of the poor can also be a way to express devotion to Jesus. But in this context, what do Judas's and the other disciples' responses reveal?

_____

_____

_____

_____

_____

_____

_____

_____

_____

_____

5. Sometimes when you focus on the "right" or "practical" way of doing ministry or worshiping God, you may judge others for not doing it the same way you would. How does this passage inform the way you should respond when you experience differences in how to worship and serve God?

_____

_____

_____

_____

_____

_____

_____

_____

6. Mary demonstrates her love for Jesus with humility and extravagance, not caring what others think of her behavior because she values Jesus above all else. She pours out perfume that costs a year's wages and then wipes Jesus' feet with her unbound hair. In what ways can you generously express your love for Jesus with your time, finances, or service regardless of what others think of you?

"In Palestine no respectable woman would ever appear in public with her hair unbound."[3] To wear one's hair down in public was considered immoral. But Mary loved Jesus so much that her love was entirely unselfconscious.

_____

_____

_____

_____

_____

_____

_____

_____

In both Matthew's and Mark's accounts of this story, Jesus says that wherever the gospel is preached throughout the world, what Mary has done will also be told in memory of her. He also calls what she's done a "beautiful" (*kalos*) thing. The Greek word *kalos* has an ethical or moral sense and can mean "beautiful," "good," or "desirable." It can refer to something that is so attractively good that it inspires others to embrace what is beautiful and praiseworthy.

7. Mary does not perform this act to gain a name for herself. However, in her humble act of devotion, Jesus not only defends Mary but also elevates her. How does Jesus commend her? (See Matthew 26:10-13; Mark 14:6-9.)

_____

_____

_____

_____

_____

_____

_____

_____

_____

_____

8. What can you learn about Mary and Jesus' relationship based on how they treat each other?

_____

_____

_____

_____

_____

_____

_____

_____

_____

_____

_____

9. Mary's beautiful act fills the house with the fragrance of perfume. In 2 Corinthians 2:14-15, Paul says that we are the "pleasing aroma of Christ" and that the fragrance of the knowledge of Christ is spread through us. Recount a time when someone did a beautiful thing without words that helped others "smell" the fragrance of the knowledge of Christ. How would you describe that fragrance?

----

10. We see Mary's growth as a worshiper in her interactions with Jesus. She starts off as a humble learner (Luke 10:38-42). In her grief, she experiences Jesus' love as He weeps with her, and then she sees Jesus' power as she witnesses her brother's miraculous resurrection (John 11:32-44). Her heart of worship deepens as she encounters Jesus' loving faithfulness at various points in her life. Describe God's steadfast love and faithfulness to you in some key moments of your life.

Your Response

Mary breaks traditional social and religious norms to be close to Jesus, bringing Him her praise and her pain. Sometimes you bring your joy and thanksgiving to God. Other times you may bring Him your sorrow, lament, and even disappointment with Him. How can you bring your full, authentic self to kneel at Jesus' feet without feeling like you need to conform to others' expectations?

_____

_____

_____

_____

_____

_____

_____

_____

_____

_____

_____

_____

_____

_____

_____

_____

_____

_____

_____

_____

For Further Study

Read Luke 7:36-50. In this passage, Jesus is anointed by a different woman, who lived a sinful life. She loves Him so much because He has forgiven her of much. How is the story in Luke similar to the story of Mary anointing Jesus? How does the Pharisee respond to that woman's actions? How does Jesus commend her?

MARY MAGDALENE

John 20:1-18

BEFORE SHE MEETS JESUS, Mary Magdalene is tormented by seven demons and probably battles daily with despair. Then Jesus heals her and sets her free from her suffering. From that moment on, Mary does not want to leave Jesus' side. She becomes His student, following Him from town to town. Defying cultural and religious norms, Jesus welcomes Mary and other women to learn alongside the men and allows the women to provide ongoing financial support for His ministry (Luke 8:1-3).

When Jesus is arrested, all the male disciples except John scatter. But Mary Magdalene and the other women who follow Jesus from Galilee courageously remain with Jesus to the end and minister to His needs (Matthew 27:55-56; Mark 15:40-41). The different Gospel accounts emphasize various women who are at the foot of the cross and at the tomb following Jesus' burial, but Mary Magdalene consistently appears in all four Gospels. As painful as it is, the women stay to bear witness as Jesus suffers and dies on the cross. They hear His last words and watch His final breath (Mark 15:40-41). When Jesus' body is taken down, the women follow to see where He is laid and then prepare spices and ointment for His body (Mark 15:47; Luke 23:55-56).

In this session, we focus on Mary Magdalene's grief at the empty tomb and her encounter with the risen Christ in John 20:1-18. Jesus appears to her first after His resurrection and gives her the joy of being the first one to share the good news of His resurrection. Because of Mary's faithfulness to Jesus in life and in death, we have "a continuous and harmonious account of Jesus's ministry, death, burial, and resurrection."[1]

1. Describe a time when you experienced something unexpectedly good or beautiful that filled you with wonder.

_____

_____

_____

_____

_____

_____

_____

_____

_____

_____

2. Read John 20:1-18. With a heavy heart, Mary returns to the tomb at her first opportunity following the Sabbath. What do you think Mary feels when she discovers that Jesus' body is missing (verses 1-2)?

_____

_____

_____

_____

_____

_____

_____

_____

_____

In verse 11, the word *klaiō* means "to weep aloud, expressing uncontainable, audible grief." The same word is used in John 11:33 when Mary of Bethany weeps over the loss of her brother Lazarus. Mary Magdalene experiences grief upon grief, seeing Jesus die and then thinking His body had been stolen.

3. Peter and John investigate the scene and then leave, but Mary stays outside the tomb to weep alone (verse 11). Through her tears, Mary bends over and looks into the empty tomb again and encounters something that she did not see before: angels. What stands out to you about how she interacts with the angels (verse 13)?

_____

_____

_____

_____

_____

_____

_____

_____

4. Mary is so overcome by grief and so focused on retrieving Jesus' body that she does not recognize Jesus when He appears to her. Describe a time when your focus on your own pain has prevented you from seeing that Jesus is with you or at work in your life.

_____

_____

_____

_____

_____

_____

_____

_____

5. In verse 16, Jesus simply says Mary's name. What does hearing Jesus say her name immediately elicit from Mary?

_____

_____

_____

_____

_____

_____

_____

_____

_____

_____

6. Jesus, the Good Shepherd, "calls his own sheep by name." The sheep listen to His voice and follow His leading (John 10:3). The prophet Isaiah wrote, "Before I was born the LORD called me; from my mother's womb he has spoken my name" (Isaiah 49:1). Have you sensed or heard God speak to you? How did that experience build your faith?

Aubrey Sampson writes, "What if, in place of the negative names in your story, God wants to speak a new name, a better name, a healing name, a loving name, a freeing name over you? And what if he already has? In God, you are named—perfectly and truly—because in him, you are known completely."[2]

_____

_____

_____

_____

_____

_____

_____

_____

_____

_____

7. Jesus tells Mary that she must not hold on to Him because He has "not yet ascended to the Father" (verse 17). It is natural to want to hang on to the version of Jesus you have known. How has your understanding of who Jesus is changed over time? In what ways can you continue to grow in that understanding?

_____

_____

_____

_____

_____

_____

_____

_____

_____

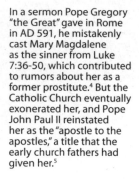

In a sermon Pope Gregory "the Great" gave in Rome in AD 591, he mistakenly cast Mary Magdalene as the sinner from Luke 7:36-50, which contributed to rumors about her as a former prostitute.[4] But the Catholic Church eventually exonerated her, and Pope John Paul II reinstated her as the "apostle to the apostles," a title that the early church fathers had given her.[5]

8. Jesus chooses to appear first to Mary Magdalene and entrusts her with the important assignment of going to tell the brothers of His risen presence (Mark 16:9; John 20:14-18). Jesus will appear to the male disciples later, but He gives Mary the honor of being the first evangelist of His resurrection, an "apostle to the apostles."[3] Why do you think He chooses her?

_____

_____

_____

_____

_____

_____

_____

_____

9. What is an assignment God has entrusted to you? In what ways can you be faithful in carrying out this assignment?

_____

_____

_____

_____

_____

_____

_____

_____

_____

_____

_____

10. In the time of Jesus, women were seen as lacking credibility in comparison to men. How does this fact give reliability to the Gospel narratives?

_____

_____

_____

_____

_____

_____

_____

_____

_____

_____

Karla Zazueta writes, "No Jewish historian wanting to fabricate a story would have chosen women as the primary witnesses. . . . God operates in fascinating ways, elevating the perceived weak and frivolous nature of women to that of valor, bringing honor to women and glory to God."[6]

11. Without hesitation, Mary goes to the disciples to
    share the news: "I have seen the Lord!" (verse 18).
    In what ways have you seen Jesus show up in your
    life? Or in what ways are you still praying for Him
    to show up?

Your Response

Describe a powerful encounter you have had with the living Jesus. If you haven't had such an experience yet, how would you like to encounter Him?

For Further Study

Read Matthew 27:55-56; Mark 15:40-41; and Luke 8:1-3. What do these female disciples, who follow, serve, support, and remain with Jesus during His crucifixion, reveal about the role of women in Jesus' ministry?

_____

_____

_____

_____

_____

_____

_____

_____

_____

_____

_____

_____

_____

_____

_____

_____

_____

_____

_____

_____

_____

_____

_____

THE WOMEN OF ROMANS 16

Romans 16:1-16

JESUS PROMISES THAT AFTER HE LEAVES He will send the Holy Spirit and that His followers will do even greater things than He did (John 14:12). And in His last words to the disciples before He ascends to heaven, Jesus says, "You will receive power when the Holy Spirit comes on you; and you will be my witnesses in Jerusalem, and in Judea and Samaria, and to the ends of the earth" (Acts 1:8). At Pentecost, God pours out the Holy Spirit on *all* people, which includes the gift of prophecy to both men and women (Acts 2:17).

After Pentecost, God uses Paul and others to spread the gospel throughout the Roman Empire. In this session, we will study the last chapter of Paul's magnum opus, the letter of Romans. Romans gives the fullest explanation in the New Testament of the life, death, and resurrection of Christ. Paul recognizes the strategic importance of the city and writes this letter to introduce himself to the Romans and prepare for an anticipated trip to visit them (Romans 15:23-24).

In the final chapter of Romans, Paul sends his personal greetings to people by name, including many women. The people he greets serve as a reference for him to the Roman churches. The greetings section contains a treasure trove of information about the status of women in ministry in the first-century church. Paul frequently gets a bad rap for his view of women based on a few verses in the Epistles, which are often used out of context. But here we see how Paul praises women as invaluable partners and leaders in his ministry. In this session, we will study the women listed in Romans 16 to learn about how women have faithfully served the church since the very beginning.

Of the twenty-seven named people, ten are women, and seven of these women are described in terms of their ministry: Phoebe, Priscilla, Mary, Junia, Tryphena, Tryphosa, and Persis. In contrast, only three men (Aquila, Andronicus, and Urbanus) are described in terms of their ministry, and two of these men are ministering alongside a female partner (Aquila with Priscilla and Andronicus with Junia).

1. Read Romans 16:1-16. What do you notice about the women named in the greetings section? What words and actions are associated with them?

_____

_____

_____

_____

_____

_____

_____

_____

_____

The Greek word *diakonon* has been translated "deacon" or "servant." It literally means "one who ministers or serves." While "deacon" can have this generalized meaning, it can also refer to the ecclesiastical office of a deacon, which is considered a position of spiritual leadership.

2. The person who carried the letter to the city would have had an important role in answering questions and ensuring that the letter was understood correctly. The letter carrier perhaps even read the letter aloud to the Roman churches for the first time. Who likely carried Paul's letter to Rome, and how does Paul commend her in verses 1-2?

_____

_____

_____

_____

_____

_____

_____

_____

_____

3. In addition to being a deacon, Phoebe is described as a "benefactor" (*prostatis*) to Paul and many others (verse 2). She was probably a financial patron or perhaps a helper in other ways. In what ways do you feel called and equipped to use your time, talent, or treasure to support God's work in the world?

_____

_____

_____

_____

_____

_____

_____

_____

4. Priscilla and Aquila were probably among the Jewish Christians who had to leave Rome after Emperor Claudius ordered the Jews to leave in AD 49. They came to Corinth and became friends with Paul as fellow tentmakers there. When Paul left Corinth, he took them with him to Ephesus (Acts 18:1 3, 18-19), where they led a house church and taught Apollos, who had gaps in his understanding of the gospel (Acts 18:24-26). How does Paul describe Priscilla and Aquila in verses 3-4?

At the time of this letter, the couple has returned to Rome and is leading a house church there (verse 5). We don't know how exactly they put their lives at risk for Paul; perhaps they intervened during a riot in Ephesus (Acts 19:23-41). But we do know that they put themselves in a situation where they could have died for Paul.

Priscilla's name is listed before Aquila's five out of the seven times they are mentioned together in Scripture. Commentators note the reason for her being named first may have been because she had greater leadership qualities, been more active in Christian ministry, or come from a higher social class than Aquila.[1]

_____

_____

_____

_____

_____

_____

_____

_____

5. Today, "tentmaker" is often used to refer to someone who performs Christian service without pay, often overseas, and who earns a living by other means. Read 1 Peter 2:9-10. As believers, we are a "royal priesthood" and in a sense are like "tentmakers" who serve in ministry regardless of our day jobs. How can you be more intentional in your daily ministry like Priscilla and Aquila?

_____

_____

_____

_____

_____

_____

_____

_____

6. Name the four women in this chapter who work hard in the Lord (verses 6, 12). In 1 Corinthians 15:58, Paul writes, "Always give yourselves fully to the work of the Lord, because you know that your labor in the Lord is not in vain." What does it look like for you to give yourself to the work of the Lord?

_____

_____

_____

_____

_____

_____

_____

_____

7. Some theologians debate whether "Junia" was meant to be translated "Junianus" (the male form of the name). Junia (*Iounian* in Greek) was a common name for women in the ancient Roman world, and early generations of Christians, including the church fathers, read it as a female name. *Iounian* "has been found six times in extrabiblical texts, and more than 250 times in inscriptions. Conversely, the suggested masculine names, *Iounías* and *Iouniâs*, have never been found in either text or inscription."[2] What do you learn about Junia, along with Andronicus, in verse 7?

> The Bible likens God to a woman giving birth, a mother bear avenging her cubs, a mother eagle hovering over its young to carry them when they fall, and a mother hen who wants to bring her brood close when trouble comes (Isaiah 42:14; Hosea 13:8; Deuteronomy 32:11-12; Matthew 23:37, respectively).

_____

_____

_____

_____

_____

_____

_____

_____

8. Junia and her partner, Andronicus, were willing to suffer for their faith in prison. You may not face the same level of persecution, but you may still face difficulties in professing your faith in Christ. What challenges do you face in sharing your Christian beliefs?

_____

_____

_____

_____

_____

_____

_____

_____

There is a translation debate about whether the Greek phrase *episēmoi en tois apostolois* means "esteemed/outstanding among the apostles" or "well-known to the apostles." The view that the pair were "distinguished as apostles among the apostles" was adopted by the early church fathers and has been "the most common view among modern commentators, endorsed by most modern translations." The view that they were "well-known to the apostles" is "grammatically possible" but not as "natural [a] reading of the Greek."[3] Regardless of whether Junia was an apostle, she was one of the earliest Jewish believers and was imprisoned for her faith along with Paul.

9. In verse 13, Paul says that Rufus's mother has been a mother to him. Not everyone will have biological children, but all of us can be spiritual mothers or be like mothers to others. When you are "mothering," regardless of whether you are a man or a woman, you reflect God's maternal qualities: nurturing, protecting, providing, bringing life. Who has been a spiritual mother or like a mother to you in your life? What would it look like for you to reflect God's maternal qualities in your relationship with a younger person in your life?

_____

_____

_____

_____

_____

_____

_____

_____

_____

10. After studying the women listed in Paul's greetings, how would you describe Paul's view of women in ministry?

_____

_____

_____

_____

_____

_____

_____

_____

_____

_____

Your Response

These early Christian women in Romans 16 exhibit genuine faith and serve God with the varied gifts and opportunities God has given them. All these women we have studied in the past sessions are part of the "great cloud of witnesses," who can encourage us to persevere and keep running the race of faith set before us (Hebrews 12:1). Of all the women we have looked at in this study, which one has encouraged you the most? Describe how this woman has inspired you to live your life differently.

_____

_____

_____

_____

_____

_____

_____

_____

_____

_____

_____

_____

_____

_____

_____

_____

_____

_____

_____

_____

_____

_____

For Further Study

Paul partners with another woman who is instrumental in establishing the first church in Philippi. Lydia of Thyatira, a successful businesswoman, is considered the first Christian convert in Europe. One Sabbath, Paul and his companions go to the riverside in Philippi and begin to speak to the women gathered there, including Lydia. When she and the members of her household are baptized, Lydia invites Paul and his companions to stay at her home and hosts them after Paul and Silas come out of prison. It is likely that the first Christian congregation in Philippi continued to meet in Lydia's home. Read Acts 16:13-15, 40. What do you learn about Lydia?

_____

_____

_____

_____

_____

_____

_____

_____

_____

_____

_____

_____

_____

_____

_____

_____

NOTES

SESSION ONE—MARY AND ELIZABETH

1. Barbara E. Reid, *Choosing the Better Part? Women in the Gospel of Luke* (Collegeville, MN: Liturgical Press, 1996), 55.
2. Richard Bauckham, *Gospel Women: Studies of the Named Women in the Gospels* (Grand Rapids, MI: Eerdmans, 2002), 55.
3. William Barclay, *The Gospel of Luke* (Philadelphia: Westminster Press, 1956), 8.
4. Kristi McLelland, *Jesus and Women: In the First Century and Now* (Nashville: Lifeway, 2019), 128–29.
5. Scot McKnight, *The Jesus Creed: Loving God, Loving Others* (Brewster, MA: Paraclete Press, 2004), 89–90.

SESSION TWO—THE SAMARITAN WOMAN

1. Lynn Cohick, "The 'Woman at the Well': Was the Samaritan Woman Really an Adulteress?," in *Vindicating the Vixens: Revisiting Sexualized, Vilified, and Marginalized Women of the Bible*, ed. Sandra Glahn (Grand Rapids, MI: Kregel Academic, 2017), 251.
2. Craig S. Keener, *The IVP Bible Background Commentary: New Testament*, 2nd ed. (Downers Grove, IL: IVP Academic, 2014), 259.
3. Caryn A. Reeder, *The Samaritan Woman's Story: Reconsidering John 4 After #ChurchToo* (Downers Grove, IL: IVP Academic, 2022), 154–55.
4. Cohick, *Vindicating the Vixens*, 251–52.
5. Christ Community Church, "3D Worship [Skye Jethani]," sermon video, October 26, 2015, https://youtu.be/a-ais5j8eWY. See 33:50–34:22.
6. Reeder, *The Samaritan Woman's Story*, 166–67. John goes on to introduce eight "I am" statements in his Gospel: I am "the bread of life"; "the light of the world"; "the gate for the sheep"; "the good shepherd"; "the resurrection and the life"; "the way and the truth and the life"; "the true vine"; and "before Abraham was born." For further study on the "I am" statements of Jesus, see the LifeChange topical study *Who Jesus Is: A Bible Study on the "I Am" Statements of Christ.*

SESSION THREE—THE BLEEDING WOMAN

1. Mary Ann Getty-Sullivan, *Women in the New Testament* (Collegeville, MN: Liturgical Press, 2001), 56.
2. Philip Yancey, *What's So Amazing about Grace?* (Grand Rapids, MI: Zondervan, 1997), 53.

3. Curt Thompson, *The Soul of Shame: Retelling the Stories We Believe about Ourselves* (Downers Grove, IL: IVP Books, 2015), 31, 35.
4. Aubrey Sampson, *Known: How Believing Who God Says You Are Changes Everything* (Colorado Springs: NavPress, 2021), 44.
5. *NIV Study Bible*, fully rev. ed. (Grand Rapids, MI: Zondervan, 2020), 1721 (note on Mark 5:34).

SESSION FOUR–THE CANAANITE WOMAN

1. Craig S. Keener, *The IVP Bible Background Commentary: New Testament*, 2nd ed. (Downers Grove, IL: IVP Academic, 2014), 85.
2. Keener, *IVP Bible Background Commentary*, 85.
3. Alice Connor, *Brave: Women of the Bible and their Stories of Grief, Mercy, Folly, Joy, Sex, and Redemption* (Minneapolis: Broadleaf Books, 2021), 156.
4. Timothy Keller, *Jesus the King: Understanding the Life and Death of the Son of God* (New York: Penguin Books, 2016), 95.
5. M. Eugene Boring, *The New Interpreter's Bible, Volume VIII: General Articles on the New Testament, the Gospel of Matthew, the Gospel of Mark* (Nashville: Abingdon Press, 1995), 328–29, 337.

SESSION FIVE–MARTHA

1. The traditional and most commonly accepted view is that Martha of Bethany in John 11 is the same Martha who hosted Jesus in her home in Luke 10. However, a doctoral student at Duke University, Elizabeth Schrader, has claimed that early manuscripts were altered and Mary (Magdalene) was changed to Martha (of Bethany), which she suggests was an attempt to minimize the legacy of Mary Magdalene. Eric Ferreri, "Mary or Martha? A Duke Scholar's Research Finds Mary Magdalene Downplayed by New Testament Scribes," June 18, 2019, Duke Today, https://today.duke.edu/2019/06/mary-or-martha-duke-scholars-research-finds-mary-magdalene-downplayed-new-testament-scribes.
2. Craig S. Keener, *The IVP Bible Background Commentary: New Testament*, 2nd ed. (Downers Grove, IL: IVP Academic, 2014), 283.
3. William Barclay, *The Gospel of John*, vol. 2 (Philadelphia: Westminster Press, 1956), 105–6.
4. Mark Vroegop, *Dark Clouds, Deep Mercy: Discovering the Grace of Lament* (Wheaton, IL: Crossway, 2019), 26.
5. *The Woman's Study Bible: Receiving God's Truth for Balance, Hope, and Transformation (NIV)* (Nashville: Thomas Nelson, 2018), 1551 (note on John 11:35).
6. Allie M. Ernst, *Martha from the Margins: The Authority of Martha in Early Christian Tradition* (Leiden, The Netherlands: Brill, 2009), 24.

SESSION SIX–MARY OF BETHANY

1. Craig S. Keener, *The IVP Bible Background Commentary: New Testament*, 2nd ed. (Downers Grove, IL: IVP Academic, 2014), 285.
2. Keener, *IVP Bible Background Commentary*, 285.
3. William Barclay, *The Gospel of John*, vol. 2 (Philadelphia: Westminster Press, 1956), 128.

SESSION SEVEN—MARY MAGDALENE

1. Karla Zazueta, "Mary Magdalene: Repainting Her Portrait of Misconceptions," in *Vindicating the Vixens: Revisiting Sexualized, Vilified, and Marginalized Women of the Bible*, ed. Sandra Glahn (Grand Rapids, MI: Kregel Academic, 2017), 270.
2. Aubrey Sampson, *Known: How Believing Who God Says You Are Changes Everything* (Colorado Springs: NavPress, 2021), xix.
3. Brandon L. Wanless, "Apostle to the Apostles," *The Sacra Doctrina Projects Thomistica* (blog), July 22, 2019, https://thomistica.net/posts/2019/7/22/apostle-to-the-apostles.
4. Gregory the Great, "Homily XXXIII," in Richard J. Hooper, *The Crucifixion of Mary Magdalene: The Historical Tradition of the First Apostle and the Ancient Church's Campaign to Suppress It* (Sedona, AZ: Sanctuary, 2005), 79–80.
5. "Apostolic Letter *Mulieris Dignitatem* of the Supreme Pontiff John Paul II on the Dignity and Vocation of Women on the Occasion of the Marian Year," Vatican.va, 1988, accessed July 15, 2022, https://www.vatican.va/content/john-paul-ii/en/apost_letters/1988/documents/hf_jp-ii_apl_19880815_mulieris-dignitatem.html#_ednref38.
6. Zazueta, *Vindicating the Vixens*, 269.

SESSION EIGHT—THE WOMEN OF ROMANS 16

1. Melanie Mar Chow, "For Better and Worse: Co-Laboring in Marriage and Ministry," in *Mirrored Reflections: Reframing Biblical Characters*, eds. Young Lee Hertig and Chloe Sun (Eugene, OR: Wipf and Stock, 2010), 113.
2. Amy Peeler, "Junia/Joanna: Heard of the Good News," in *Vindicating the Vixens: Revisiting Sexualized, Vilified, and Marginalized Women of the Bible*, ed. Sandra Glahn (Grand Rapids, MI: Kregel Academic, 2017), 276–77.
3. Richard Bauckham, *Gospel Women: Studies of the Named Women in the Gospels* (Grand Rapids, MI: Eerdmans, 2002), 172.

MAKE DISCIPLESHIP
A LIFESTYLE

THE 2:7 SERIES..
Discipleship training with a proven track record

DESIGN FOR DISCIPLESHIP...
Over 7 million sold

THE WAYS OF THE ALONGSIDER...
For small groups, classes, or one-on-one discipling